EVO HEYNING

co-authored with GENE

REALITYCRAFT PRESENTS

GUIDEBOOK

PROMPTCRAFT

PROMPTCRAFT
GUIDEBOOK

Writing Generative Prompts for Creative Work

EVO HEYNING

2023   REALITYCRAFT MEDIA

FIRST EDITION   Q1 2023   EVO.IST

ISBN: 9798374946079

CONTENTS

1
INTRODUCTION TO PROMPTCRAFT

Concepts of promptcraft
Artistry and creativity in prompting
Prompt structure and experiments in this guidebook

2
PROMPT ENGINEERING BASICS

Different types of prompts and their uses
Strategic communications and making choices for prompt development
Tips for finding inspiration and generating new ideas through prompts

3
PROMPT CREATIVITY

Definition of prompt engineering and how PE informs strategy at work
Designing and refining prompts to achieve specific creative outcomes
Prompt engineering adjacent to other creative fields

4
ARTS & CREATIVE

Prompts to enhance artistic expression and creativity
Different types of art prompts and their applications
Evolution of copyright, intellectual property and diffusion models

5
SECRET RECIPES

Generating new story ideas and characters
Using prompts to develop plot, dialogue, and setting
Writing prompts and adapting elements for applications in different genres

6
TIPS & TOOLS

Generative music composition and performance
Promptcraft in design and architectural ideation
Concept and asset development for storytelling, video, gaming, interactive media and film

Tools, recipes and open source resource guides to share
Promptcraft and Realitycraft: using prompts to design and be creative in daily life
Resources for learning more about promptcraft and generative media

PROMPTCRAFT

TRY ON A NEW STYLE

ITERATE OVER TIME WITH EXPERIMENTATION

This book is written using a mix of generative art and media tools including Midjourney, ChatGPT, DALL-E, Stable Diffusion, Canva, Playground.AI, Scenario.gg, Simulacra.io, Nightcafe and includes tests with dozens of algorithmic generators. Images and text are unedited to give useful insight on progress. In some cases, areas are included to add your own notes on your experiments. Try it & take notes.

media makes the message that makes the media, that remixes the messages

Promptcraft: Generated in Stable Diffusion - DreamStudio

PROMPTCRAFT is a creative process to design and realize your generative ideas into works

Using Words, Images & Numbers

Promptcraft: Image in Midjourney V4

USING THIS GUIDEBOOK

Promptcraft as a guidebook provides a starting place for building a comprehensive collection of language tools for developing prompts that can be used to inspire and guide the creative process in any medium.

These prompts are designed to be flexible and adaptable and can be used in a variety of ways depending on the needs of the creators.

Not every prompt or experiment will work with every generative tool, your mileage and generations will vary. If you hit an error, try again in a new way.

Promptcraft: Image in Midjourney V4

Exercises in this book include projects you can try at home or with colleagues at work in your ideation sessions. Some of these generative tools may be baked into programs you are already using. Check into the generative tools in your creative suites and software at work.

Promptcraft: Text to Image generator in Canva, Abstract Mode

GENERATIVE
TOOLS
EXPLORED

GENERATING IMAGES

Text to Image generators such as Midjourney, Stable Diffusion and DALL-E

CHAT, TEXT & WRITING

Tools useful for writing fiction or nonfiction content including Copy.AI, ChatGPT and Jasper.AI

VIDEO, 3D & WORLDBUILDING

Emerging software for 3D asset prompting, video creation and generators built into existing creative suites for designers

Generative tools are used in a variety of fields, including art, design, writing, and music to try new ideas and spark inspiration. In this guide we will explore the different types of creative media prompts and their uses and discuss a variety of AI creative tools that can be used to generate media.

Image-based prompting generators seen above are commonly described as "AI art" tools but are can also be described as diffusion machine learning tools. Images and words serve as a starting point for generating new ideas through the formation of prompts. Prompts and images can be used to generate endless ideas for writing, art, design, and other creative projects. Popular 2D image-based prompting tools like Midjourney, Stable Diffusion and DALL-E are compared in this guidebook for promptcraft; 3D images are in alpha.

Text-based prompts consist of a single word, phrase, or sentence that serves as a starting point for generating new ideas. Text prompts can be used to generate ideas for writing, art, design, and other creative projects. Some popular text-based prompts are used for writing business or media copy, quick scripts or exploring questions like "What if," "Imagine," and "Create a story about."

Sound: Prompting for Music

Sound-based prompts prompt by text or use sound clips to inspire new ideas. Text prompts that may include known songs, genres or artists can be used to query databases and generate ideas for music, sound design, and other audio-based projects. Others may sample based on an artist or sound upload. Popular sound-based prompts are used for sound effects, ambient sounds, livestreaming backgrounds and music tracks. MyNoise.net is an ambient generator that has been around for years; prompt-generated music tools such as MuseNet from OpenAI are now accessible and out of beta.

Video-based prompts

Video-based prompting can use text, GIFs, clips and moving images to inspire new ideas. These prompts can be used to generate video clips, textures for film, animation, cinematics and other video-based projects. Popular video-based prompts include short films, animations and music videos; the Augie from AugXLabs is explored in this guidebook while advanced tools may take a few more years to reach public use. NVIDIA has provided tools for professional filmmaking generative work for years.

Prompting 3D Assets & Worlds

While a few popular AI-based creative tools have created demos where text to worldbuilding or text to 3D generation is available, few tools are publically accessible yet. NVIDIA's Get3D was released in 2022 while other tools like Simulacra allow for 2D generative work in Stable Diffusion to happen socially in a 3D web browser. Companies like NVIDIA provide professional enterprise-level AI tools for production.

How does the process of writing a prompt engage creative play?

Creativity can be defined as the ability to come up with a mix of ideas and transform them into something new. Creating engages our ability to think outside the box, experiment and see things in new and different ways. In promptcraft, creativity comes through describing our imagination and inquiry in accessible ways, engaging questions and thought-provoking ideas while connecting styles, stories and ideas into new works to inspire and transform over time and iteration. This type of creativity can be collective, communal and remixable.

Prompting begins a process of creative iteration and discovery you can take into any arena

How does promptcraft engage a process of artistry?

Promptcraft Cat: Scenario Photo: Evo Heyning

Artistry engages human expression, a capacity to create something that is beautiful, meaningful, thought-provoking or special. A process of artistry is more than crafting a thing of beauty; artistry is a valued process of discovery, taking inspiration from the world around us or our wildest imaginations to transform ideas into something new and original. Artistry as a process creates more than something aesthetically pleasing to another person -- the process focuses attention on inquiries and concepts with meaning and purpose in our lives.

The experiment is part of the artistry. In promptcraft, artistry can be literal or conceptual as prompts are formed that are engaging and thought-provoking. These works may also have the potential to inspire or transform the ideas of the person experiencing them.

Generative or Gens or GenAI art all refer to the class of tools commonly referred to in media as "AI Art" tools such as Midjourney, Stable Diffusion and DALL-E. Additional image prompting tools like Text to Image in Canva explored here are built into larger creative toolkits. Each of these tools has unique grammar, syntax and capabilities. Image generators use text and some characters in prompts to generate new images, often engaging diffusion models in their programming. Some use apps or preset styles, others are web-based tools with great flexibility.

Many generators use images for reference. What works in one tool may not work elsewhere.

Text to Image generator in Canva

Throughout the book, there are examples and case studies of prompts that have been successfully used in various writing contexts as well as exercises and prompts to try on your own or with your team at work. Your mileage may vary. Experiment wildly.

Text to Image generator in Canva

To tap into your own creativity in the process of developing prompts, it helps to start by getting in touch with your own thoughts and feelings. This can be done through journaling, meditation or other forms of self-reflection. It helps to spend time exploring the world around us and taking inspiration from the things we see, hear, and experience. Try noting a few quality words and descriptors when reading, listening to music, relaxing or in nature.

Take a few minutes to chill out, indoors or out. Then write down the first words that come to mind.

Photo: Evo

To get closer to your ideas, iterate.
Generate & regenerate again.
Try similar ideas, 100 different ways.

Promptcraft in
Midjourney

The road to success starts with many
generations that are not yet there.

Note: The next few pages will summarize the tech inside "AI media generators" at a basic level. Feel free to skip ahead at your own pace and refer to the Promptcraft wiki for further reading.

Prompt Engineering Basics

Prompt engineering involves the creation, development and modification of generative media tools, prompts training models and modifiers to aid in the refinement of a strategic concept development process. Prompt engineers work between software tools and proprietary, open source or procedural code with internal creators and workflows, assets and tools. They may work between teams or across fields such as media production to form a bridge between concept development and production teams to assist in the creation of new ideas, concepts, and products by providing a structured and iterative process for generating creative content.

Prompt engineering is an important skill set for production and strategic concept development as it allows teams to quickly and efficiently generate a large number of ideas and concepts to match their production goals. This can be efficient and useful in industries where new ideas, content assets and products are in high demand such as advertising. By using generative media tools, businesses can reduce the time and resources required to generate new ideas, allowing them to focus on refinement, editorial cadence and other aspects of the media development process.

The emerging field of prompt engineering has its roots in artificial intelligence, machine learning and natural language processing along with software engineering and asset management in workflows such as animation and VFX.

Prompt engineering involves the use and modification of algorithms and software, data sets and training models either run locally or on the cloud that respond to user input in a generative and meaningful way. The engineer learns how to mix these tools and workflows effectively for any sort of production needs. These tools can be used to generate text, images, videos and other forms of media and can be applied in a wide range of industries, including advertising, livestreaming, venues and entertainment arenas such as gaming and toy development.

A few of these media refinement tools have been embedded in our media programs for years and others engage open source code recently available to developers using Javascript, Python, Rust, TensorFlow or in software like Blender. Code for these tools can now be prompted using OpenAI's ChatGPT to write new open source code.

Prompting in daily work and creative practice involves the process of writing and manipulating prompts in order to achieve a specific creative goal. This can involve fine-tuning of existing prompts or creating new bots, commands or tools from scratch. Prompt engineering as a field brings together prompting and creative skills with approaches to refining workflows, data sets and tools to the specific needs of the creative team and the project they are working on; refining the queries, models, training new systems and implementing how these tools and procedural code applications are assembled for optimal effects.

This guidebook is designed for prompters getting started and will not go into great detail into the engineering, technology and fine-tuning of new models for professional prompt engineering. To refine your promptcraft this guide will focus on the elements of promptcraft related to creative media experiments. Exercises explore parameters, weights and measures along with remixing and training to receive a more effective outcome from a mix of tools.

For further reading on the computer science and engineering behind AI & algorithmic creative tools, a reading list will be provided at the end of this guide and on the Github wiki.

Promptcraft as a term is used here in creative exploration to describe forming vivid and imaginative scenarios, stories or evocative situations that generate media. This generative output may elicit an emotional response and inspire creative thinking.

This definition of promptcraft includes writing text prompts, visual prompts, videos or other forms of characterized inspiration that evoke a sense of wonder, curiosity or intrigue.

The practice of promptcraft can take many forms, from writing prompts that challenge writers to explore new perspectives, to visual prompts that challenge artists to create new works of art, to storytelling prompts that inspire listeners to imagine fantastic new worlds. Whether it is a single word, a phrase, a photograph, or a piece of artwork, promptcraft is a process of sparking the imagination and inspiring creativity.

This process applied to generative art and media tools starts an inquiry, a big question. Designing the big question starts the query to /imagine then writing the prompt to that imagination.

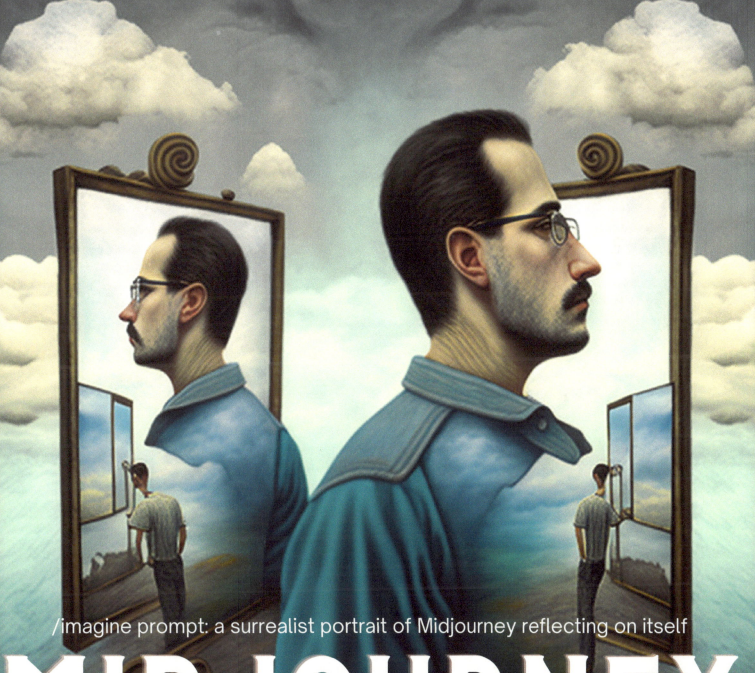

/imagine prompt: a surrealist portrait of Midjourney reflecting on itself

MIDJOURNEY

A prompt in Midjourney is a series of words, numbers and other characters that express an idea that can be generated. Your prompt can include emoji, images, words and numbers to express a mix of ideas. A prompt can be a single word or 50, there are some limits and those limits vary based on the tool.

Prompts can include a mix of characters that speak to most if not all of these elements you wish to generate:

Content type
Description
Style
Composition
Parameters

/imagine prompt:

/imagine creates an image based on the prompt text you provided. It produces a grid of 4 images, taking around 50 seconds with default settings in Midjourney. In the dialogue chat window with the Midjourney bot you can form your prompt and receive your generative media back within a minute to upscale or create a variation set.

Time to generate media will usually vary from a few seconds to a few minutes.

3 ELEMENTS OF A PROMPT IN MIDJOURNEY

/imagine There are endless possibilities...

/imagine prompt https://example/tulip.jpg https://example/tulip2.jpg a field of tulips in the style of Mary Blair --no farms --iw .5 --ar 3:2

Image Prompt   Text Prompt   Parameters

IMAGE
TEXT PROMPT
(Description, Style)
PARAMETERS

GENERATION EXPERIMENT: START WITH 3 WORDS YOU LIKE THAT MAY NOT HAVE ANYTHING TO DO WITH EACH OTHER BUT SPEAK TO A CONCEPT YOU HAVE IN YOUR MIND

TRY: ONE VAGUE, ONE STYLE & ONE EVOCATIVE WORD

EXAMPLE: CONFUSED SURREALIST DRIPPING

TYPE: /imagine prompt: _____ your words here

GETTING STARTED: WRITE A PROMPT

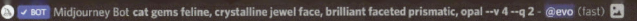
Midjourney Bot ✓ BOT Today at 10:36 AM
3D cat gems feline, crystalline jewel face, brilliant faceted prismatic, opal, unreal engine render --v 4 --q 2 - Remix by @evo (fast)

VARIATIONS

V1 V2 V3 V4

U1	U2	U3	U4	
V1	V2	V3	V4	

Choose which of the images you may want to see variations on, and REMIX your variations to fine tune what you want to see more or less of in your work

Midjourney Bot ✓ BOT Today at 10:36 AM
3D cat gems feline, crystalline jewel face, brilliant f

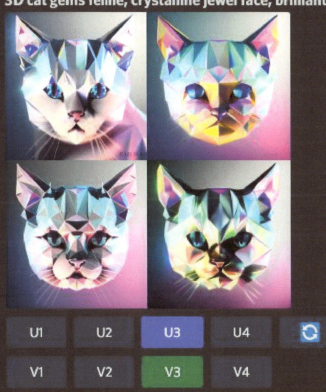

U1	U2	U3	U4
V1	V2	V3	V4

/imagine prompt: Photograph of a field of flowers at sunset with a woman running in the background, insanely detailed, cinematic lighting, 70mm, --v 4

Promptcraft is the process of writing or forming a generative prompt (text such as words, characters or emoji) to create a new media output.

Crafting a prompt will trigger the software to use algorithms on data sets, informing trained models using machine learning programs such as diffusion. This generates media through steps of natural language processing, a digital process of translating and turning your language and characters into a new set of translated works. Prompting as a craft can be used to generate creative content such as stories, poems, visual art, music, interactive experiences such as games and simulations, or handle business writing such as blog posts and ad copy.

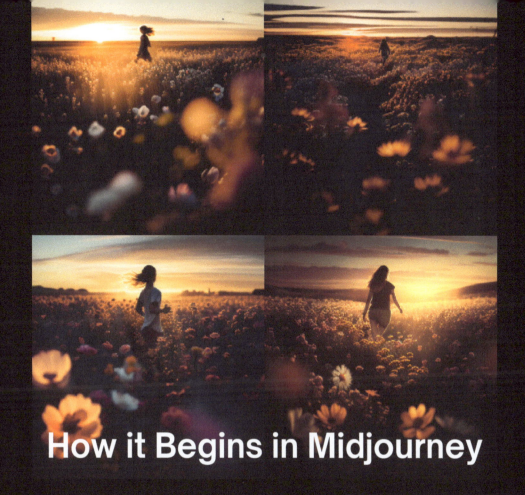

How it Begins in Midjourney

Write a /imagine prompt
Get back a group of 4 images
Pick something to work with
Remix, iterate, try again
Upscale your favorite
Take it out to repaint it
Edit in your graphic tools
Use that image in a new way

On average it takes 5-10 generations, remixes and variations to get
from a first idea to a "finished" concept ready for external edits

Photograph of a **field of poppy superbloom flowers at sunset** with an **older Indian woman running away in the background**, detailed California poppies flowers in front, **cinematic lighting, 70mm** --q 2 --v 4

Type of Media
Descriptors
Focal points
Style & Composition
Algo Modifiers

Promptcraft in Midjourney V4

This /imagine prompt has five basic elements. Detail adds to the image.

Type of Media
Descriptors
Focal points
Style Directionals
Algo Modifiers

/imagine prompt: A type of media like **painting** of a described scene such as **woman of mystery** with a **black cat on lap**, in a room from **year 1901**, **old sepia film, 8mm** --no phone --q 2 --v 4

Your generations will vary and no two will be the same unless using the exact same seed with the same prompt in the same version of the same generative tool

An image prompt or IMG2IMG uses an image in the prompt to generate new media content. Some tools can use many images for reference in generative iteration.

Locate the URL of your favorite media or upload it to the tool

Use that reference image in a new prompt that includes a new style or descriptors

Try variations on styles or combining more than 2 modifiers to shift the imagination

Upscale, Remix, Repeat, Animate

IMAGE PROMPTS

IMG2IMG

/imagine prompt: <imageurl.jpg> ____prompt____

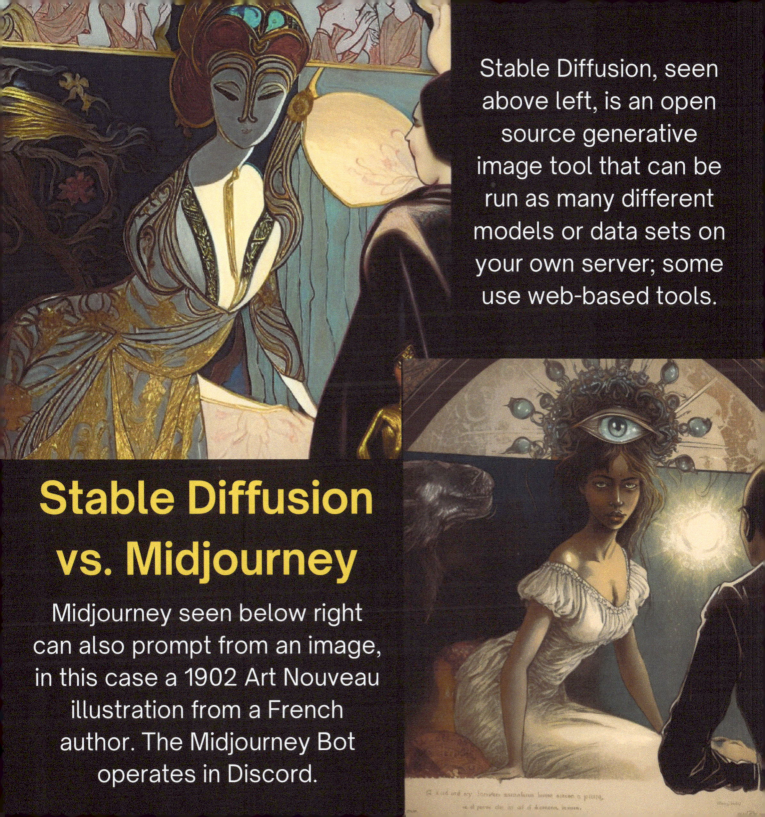

Stable Diffusion, seen above left, is an open source generative image tool that can be run as many different models or data sets on your own server; some use web-based tools.

Stable Diffusion vs. Midjourney

Midjourney seen below right can also prompt from an image, in this case a 1902 Art Nouveau illustration from a French author. The Midjourney Bot operates in Discord.

Generative content can change based on the viewer, the transformer and version, the modifiers, the model trained and the seed

Promptcraft in Stable Diffusion of art from a French Art Nouveau Political Zine, 1902

Prompts can be used in a variety of ways depending on the medium and the needs of the creator.

In writing new media work prompts can be used to generate ideas for characters, settings, storylines and plots such as this story about media sharing & mobile devices.

In visual art, prompts can be used to explore different art styles, color palettes, textures, and composition choices like "stained glass" here.

This can also inform concept & character design.

Promptcraft in Midjourney V4

Forming Language

How does promptcraft work to generate images and how is it a new type of language?

A prompt or imagination command like /imagine in Midjourney is a combination of uniquely formed characters that can query (ask!) data sets and algorithms about specific instructions in the parameters. This inquiry uses a mix of natural language processing with code that's often unseen but working inside the tool to turn your text into a generative output. **Forming this type of prompt or inquiry can be a creative or poetic experience as prompts are written with the intention of providing fragments of inspiration.**

These fragments can then be used to create something new and unique. Promptcraft is a process of taking this language and shaping it to form new types of media that may be a combination of original ideas with the diffused discoveries of the collective intelligence. The language of prompting a generator is the language of possibility, exploration, discovery and creativity, an experimental dance where the unexpected is the expected.

USE FEWER WORDS, WISELY

Descriptive Clusters of Adjectives with a Noun, Separate Objects by Commas

One strong verb for action scenes, vivid detail to backgrounds and settings

MATCH YOUR PROMPT & AUDIENCE WITH YOUR AUTHORSHIP, CREATOR TOOLING AND GOALS TO MAKE SURE YOUR GENERATIVE WORK FITS IN AND LANDS

Borrowed and riffed language from other creative communities, i.e. Rainbowcore, Glitch/Mod or Trends & Experiment with emoji to go abstract

IMAGE COMPS

People writing and drawing around a collaborative work table, pens and paper in hands

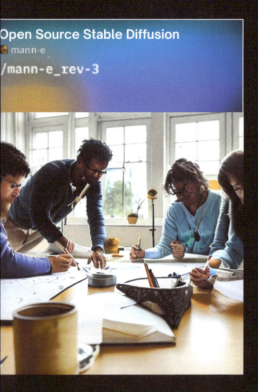

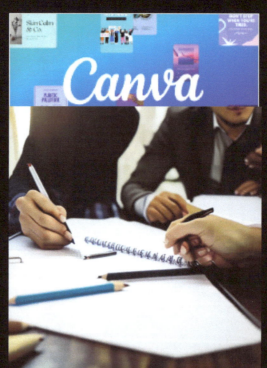

In this sample exercise three similar generators were used with the same prompt, asking for a photo generated with the text above. Each has its own focal point, flavor and detail along with accuracy on things like hands. **Try a prompt for creative work in 3 different tools to see what generates.**

ALGO MODS

Common paramaters to be modified include aspect ratio, format, chaos, negative weights (or things to not include in the generation) to bend the output and final version upscaled for use.

ALGORITHMIC MODIFIERS ARE USED TO IMPROVE THE OUTPUTS AND GENERATIVE WORKS BEFORE UPSCALING.

TOOLS & MEASURES

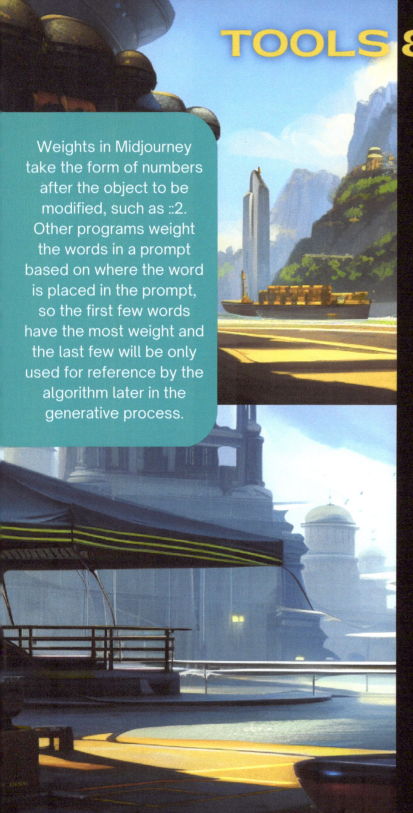

Weights in Midjourney take the form of numbers after the object to be modified, such as ::2. Other programs weight the words in a prompt based on where the word is placed in the prompt, so the first few words have the most weight and the last few will be only used for reference by the algorithm later in the generative process.

Weights and measures affect how parameters used in promptcraft refine the emphasis of what language is given the most "weight" or attention when sending a prompt to be generated. These weights are in numbers and in tools like Midjourney usually appear at the end of a word such as ::2 (with a value .5-5) after a prompted set of images, text and other parameters.

Promptcraft has a unique grammar and syntax for generating media content from a set of parameters. **Parameters are set through weights, measures and markers which are then applied to a generator's algorithms in what are known as algorithmic modifiers.** These breaks & mods often appear at the end of a prompt, through punctuation like::.

The generator tool such as Midjourney or another image generator then takes these multi-prompt breaks, numbers and parameters and creates unique content based on the nouns and descriptive words in the prompt combined with the weights and measures provided for emphasis.

Parameters to adjust in prompt through weights & measures (in Midjourney)

Chaos, Aspect Ratio, Number of Steps, Version of Model to Query, Quality and Style Modifiers, Creative modifiers like --tile or --video for autoformatted repeating patterns or --seed to generate on a specific set of training data. Toggling your use of tools (especially seed/style) can assist in worldbuilding.

Parameters are used for workflows in 3D Design and Physics Simulators as Well as Other Fields:

Volume (e.g. volume level, sound intensity)
Time (e.g. duration, frequency)
Distance (e.g. proximity, range)
Temperature (e.g. temperature setting, heat intensity)
Speed (e.g. rotation speed, velocity)
Weight (e.g. load capacity, mass)
Pressure (e.g. air pressure, force)
Brightness (e.g. light intensity, luminosity)
Density (e.g. concentration, mass per unit volume)
Angle (e.g. tilt angle, rotation angle)

In generative image and media creation, the term "Chaos" refers to the use of random or unpredictable elements in the creation process. This can include using random numbers or algorithms to generate shapes, colors, or other visual elements. The term "Seed" refers to a starting point or initial input that is used to generate the final image and reconnects the prompt to a generative source in the model. This can include a specific set of parameters or a starting image set of data that is used as a reference for the generative process. Together, chaos and seed refer to controlling the balance between randomness and control in the creation of generative images.

TRY A SEED + WEIGHTS

Use a seed to keep the same composition for a series of generations

::1.x or more

Add this weight to a phrase in your prompt to prioritize or emphasize any changes in style you are making

✓ BOT Midjourney Bot crystalline house 🏡🏠🎨💎🌄🗿 **gorgeous home natural light shines through faceted prismatic layers rooms levels prism labradorite matrix quartz modern environment, cinematic 8k,**
Job ID: 67061328-6e21-449b-a987-d7dbfdf68298
Seed: 15642

HOW SEEDS REGENERATE

**Send the envelope emoji to Midjourney
Copy the Seed (--seed #######)
Pick 1 of the 4 Variations to Upscale**

Give feedback ☺, send the envelope emoji ,
Copy the seed (note & record your seeds)
Rinse, repeat for 6-7 iterations to train that
name to the character description and features

Keeping track of your most
effective seeds will help build
consistency for composition,
storytelling and worldbuilding

Designing Characters

/imagine prompt:
Character name, character description, scene description, --seed #

Iterate, Seed, Remix

Styles to Try

Experiment

Use These Words
8-Bit, 16-Bit
Octane Render
Unreal Engine or Game Engines
Knolling or Graphic Layouts
Unusual Materials
Historic Schools of Art
Cinematic Action Directions
Die-Cut, Sticker, Logo
Graphic Design Trends
Infographic, Typography
Photography Words
Graphic Design Trends
Arcane Art Styles

70mm, 35mm, 28mm Lens
Closeup or Background
Portrait or Full Body
Landscape or Environment
Cinematic, Firelight, Neon or
Natural Lighting
Time of Day, i.e. Dusk
8K, HD, UltraHD, Detailed
Emoji for Mood, Expression
Tone & Vibe Words
Schematics & Breakdowns
List 10 Nouns to Map
Design Websites, Products
Use all Emoji in a Prompt

RIFF JAM

Promptcraft in groups is a bit like improv jazz, a type of creative flow state that happens in tandem with others using the same language in the dance as phrases, words, images and characters riff off each other to inspire and guide the creative process. Created and riffed prompt words can be useful in any medium, from writing to visual art, and are designed to stimulate the imagination and help creators generate new ideas and concepts. It is common for experiments in prompts to be shared openly to try new methods, styles, themes and design motifs. Visit art sites to learn new words others are using in your favorite images.

TOOLS VARY

Diffusion transformer models and StyleGAN tools generate images in different ways - here's a quick bit into how models & prompts work

Stable Diffusion is a text-to-image model that uses a *frozen CLIP ViT-L/14 text encoder* to tune the model to your text prompt. This encoding separates imaging elements into a *diffusion* process that starts with noise and gradually improves the image until it is entirely free of noise, progressively approaching the provided text description. Stable Diffusion is powered by Latent Diffusion Model (LDM), a text-to-image synthesis method. Diffusion models power many of the most popular generative text to image programs and differ from other forms of AI that use other methods of computing and processing to achieve generative goals.

Diffusion models (DM) such as Midjourney and Stable Diffusion are transformer-based generative models that take data and add noise over time until it is not recognizable. From that point the program will try reconstructing the image to its original form to discover how to generate pictures or other data. DMs are powerful but very computationally heavy to run for large images and media; this is why these tools will generally come at a higher cost. Your mileage may vary with subscription services and computing time provided vs. running open source solutions on your own server.

A StyleGAN such as NVIDIA's StyleGAN-1, StyleGAN-2 and StyleGAN-3 form what is called a generative adversarial network (GAN) that is specifically designed for generating media. It is trained to send back new media by learning the style and structure of a training set bespoke to that use case. StyleGANs can be used to generate a wide variety of images, from photographs of faces to abstract patterns, by manipulating the generated images. The training computing power, processing and outputs along with the process for prompting these outputs will vary depending on the complexity of the media. These assets or generations of output are rendered in highest quality for VFX, HD video and film and may include thousands of images used in the building of a scene or world. Elaborate generative works engaging complex math can take days to render and complete.

New tools like Playground.AI and Stable Diffusion can use extensions like **Instruct Pix2Pix**, available in Hugging Face for those who want to experiment with swapping out an aspect of an image for anything else.

This is a form of repainting or swapping of content is considered a style transfer, a form of generative media that was only available to VFX filmmakers until recently. Style Transfer apps are very common now and are quickly becoming a part of a release strategy with new releases.

"Make it Paris"   "Make it Hong Kong"   "Make it Manhattan"   "Make it Prague"

"Make it evening"   "Put them on roller skates"   "Turn this into 1900s"   "Make it underwater"

"Make it Minecraft"   "Turn this into the space age"   "Make them into Alexander Calder sculptures"   "Make it a Claymation"

Promptcraft by Daniel Nest   details at his blog https://www.whytryai.com/p/instructpix2pix

GENERATIVE TOOLS INSIDE
CREATIVE TOOLS YOU ARE ALREADY USING

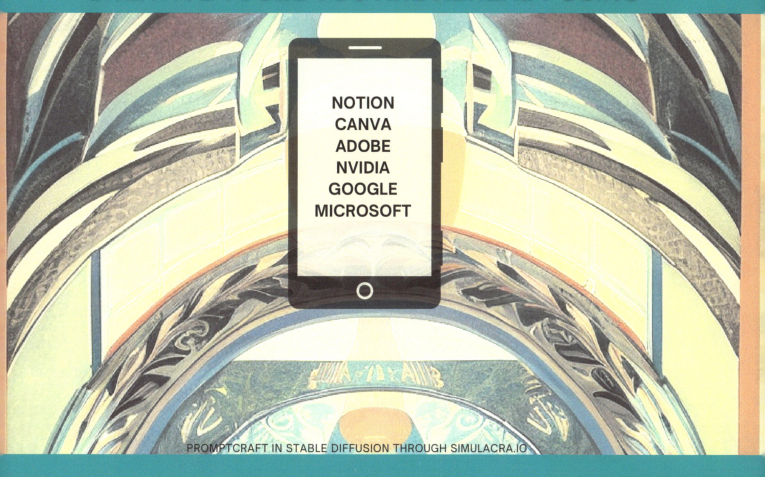

NOTION
CANVA
ADOBE
NVIDIA
GOOGLE
MICROSOFT

PROMPTCRAFT IN STABLE DIFFUSION THROUGH SIMULACRA.IO

As larger tech companies acquire access to the technology inside many of the new generative tools, these tools are finding their way into our daily lives through our creative workflows in tools we already use such as Canva and Notion.

MAGIC WRITE & TEXT TO IMAGE

Built into Canva

"ambient wash of watery colors"

Canva's generator crafted an image in less than 15 seconds, inserted that image in this book within a minute to make the background for this page.

PROMPTCRAFT IN MIDJOURNEY ON THE PROMPT: POSTER

Promptcraft tools can be specified to help with ideation in the early stages of a concept development process. For example, Midjourney here can be used to generate posters for advertising campaigns, to create storyboards for film and television projects or to generate product package designs and ideas for new products. Text generating tools can also be used to generate conceptual content for locations, campaigns, websites, social media and other digital productions

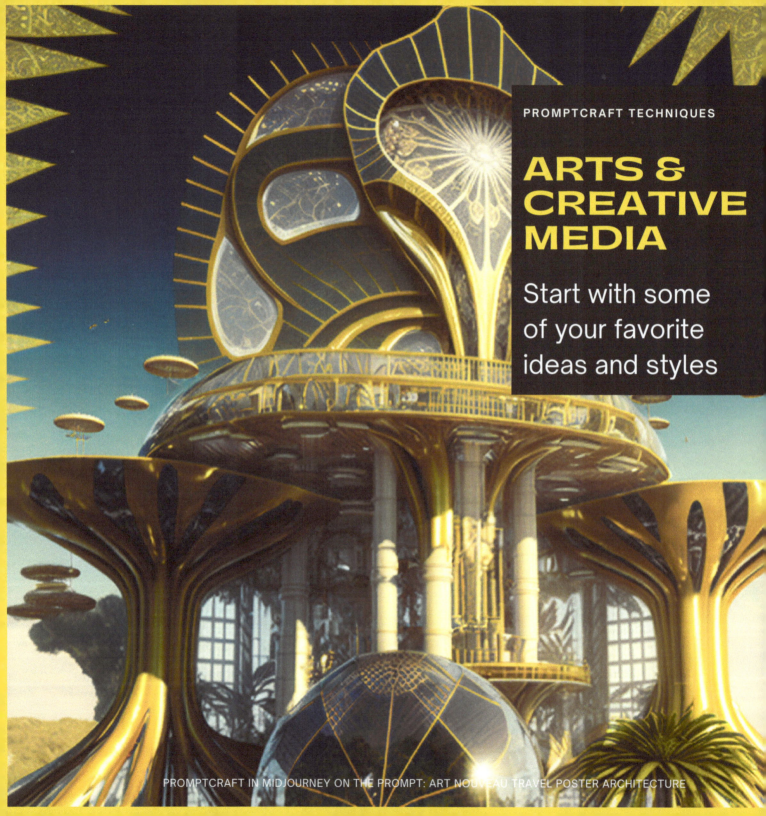

PROMPTCRAFT TECHNIQUES

ARTS & CREATIVE MEDIA

Start with some of your favorite ideas and styles

PROMPTCRAFT IN MIDJOURNEY ON THE PROMPT: ART NOUVEAU TRAVEL POSTER ARCHITECTURE

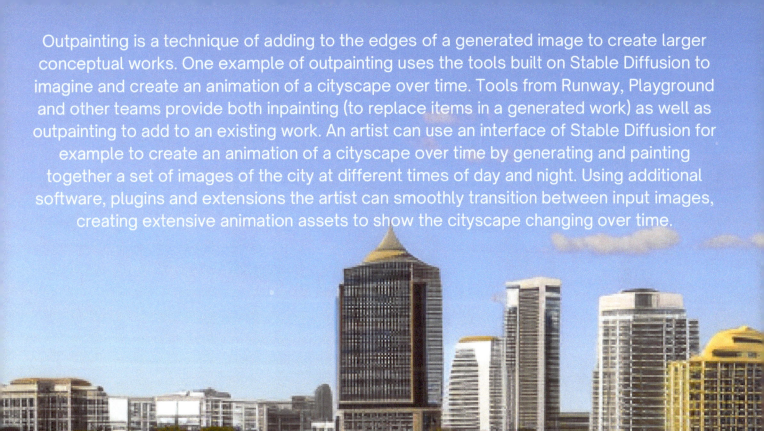

Outpainting is a technique of adding to the edges of a generated image to create larger conceptual works. One example of outpainting uses the tools built on Stable Diffusion to imagine and create an animation of a cityscape over time. Tools from Runway, Playground and other teams provide both inpainting (to replace items in a generated work) as well as outpainting to add to an existing work. An artist can use an interface of Stable Diffusion for example to create an animation of a cityscape over time by generating and painting together a set of images of the city at different times of day and night. Using additional software, plugins and extensions the artist can smoothly transition between input images, creating extensive animation assets to show the cityscape changing over time.

INPAINTING OUTPAINTING & ANIMATION

CREATIVE CURATION

Worldbuilding requires organizational tools beyond what's provided inside tools like Midjourney. Build collections, export and use them to train new models.

Curate carefully from hundreds of generations to get the most effective results long term.

Assemble bodies of work in a single image by listing those descriptive words in order of their importance - or use weights and measures to emphasize specific elements. Use your portfolio tools & publish collections or animated works from your curated works online.

generative art preview

art museum catalog

A COLLECTION OF OUR FAVORITE WORKS

Compiled by Evo with Midjourney

Gen Costs Vary Wildly

Try BlueWillow
DreamStudio
OpenJourney
Diffusion.Land
Playground.ai

Training your model or
hosting your own generative
outputs on your own server
at home/office may be more
cost effective than using a
cloud-based subscription
service. Try new tools,
they're often free to start.

Keep researching open source
solutions as they emerge

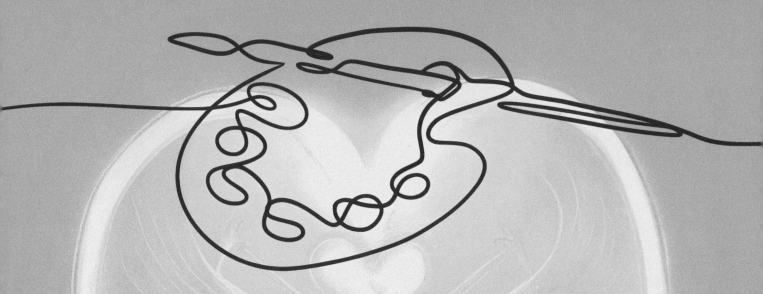

TOOLS & TIPS

**CREATE THE WORLDS
YOU WANT TO LIVE IN**

FROM THE PROMPTCRAFT WORKSHOPS

TIPS FOR PROMPTCRAFT

Use clear Nouns & Verbs

Adjectives for Descriptors

Year + Date to evoke a time

Modify Words with Weights

Give Characters Names*

Juxtapose Moods, Styles, Concepts

Track Useful Composition Seeds

Be Explicit about Palette & Design

Use Direction Words for Scenes

*try this in Midjourney or ChatGPT writing

Tips for Text-Prompts from the MidJourney Team

Anything left unsaid may surprise you

Try to be clear about any context or details that are important to you

Try visually well-defined objects

Strong feelings or mystical-sounding themes also work great

Try describing a style

Try invoking a particular medium

If the style is unspecified, it will lean towards photorealism

Speak in positives. Avoid negatives

Specify what you want clearly

If you want a specific composition, say so!

Too many small details may overwhelm the system:

Avoid: "a monkey on roller skates juggling razor blades in a hurricane"

Try: "a monkey that's a hurricane of chaos" (*or build the prompt in stages and steps -evo*)

Try taking two well defined concepts and combining them in ways no one has seen before

Try to use singular nouns or specific numbers

No razor blades to see here - too much detail

Monkey on skates was the complexity limit

Use a Notebook or Prompt Locker to Track Seeds, Prompts & Parameters over Time

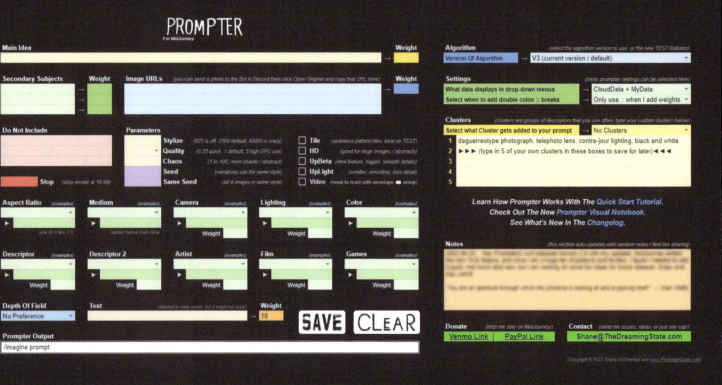

There are a number of free and open source tools emerging for tracking your progress. Try the new open source tools and donate to their makers if you find them useful like Shane from Prompter Guide. Worksheets like this can help you track hundreds of seeds and prompts over time and project iterations.

RESOURCES

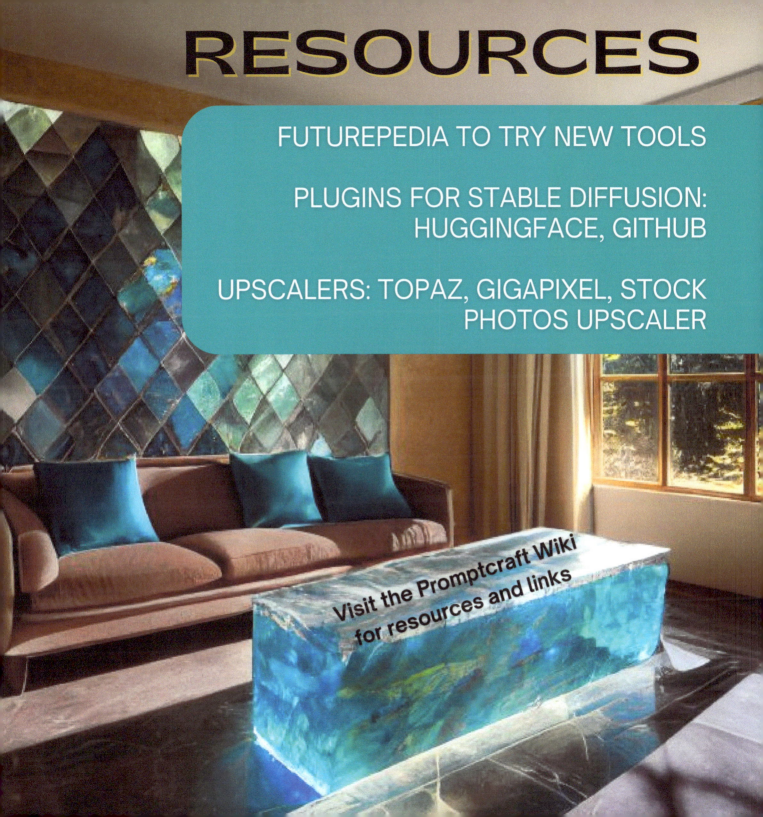

FUTUREPEDIA TO TRY NEW TOOLS

PLUGINS FOR STABLE DIFFUSION:
HUGGINGFACE, GITHUB

UPSCALERS: TOPAZ, GIGAPIXEL, STOCK
PHOTOS UPSCALER

Visit the Promptcraft Wiki
for resources and links

Quiairy

The generative tool is never going to know what you want to write here unless you tell it exactly how to deliver what you want.

PROMPTS FOR WRITING NEW MEDIA

TEXT GEN

WORKING WITH PROMPTED TEXT GENERATORS

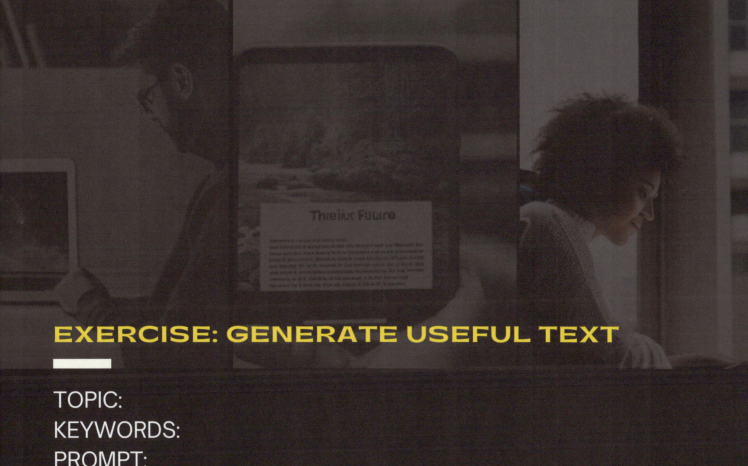

EXERCISE: GENERATE USEFUL TEXT

TOPIC:

KEYWORDS:

PROMPT:

What are you asking to write? (chapter, exercise, recipe, outline....)

Can you describe the scene in a few words?

Are there parameters, identifiers that will improve output?

Generate based on the prompt and regenerate text until it's useful

Edit, copy, paste, regenerate and edit again until it's right and ready

Take a few minutes to write out your prompt topic and goal, note a few keywords, then fill in the gaps with the style of writing you're looking for, descriptive words and detail to improve what you receive from your generative text tool of choice.

ChatGPT is a powerful language generation model developed by OpenAI that can be used to generate human-like text. However, to get the best results from ChatGPT, it is important to use the right keywords and special words

Keywords for ChatGPT:

1. "question" - When used in a prompt, ChatGPT will generate a response in the form of a question.
2. "summarize" - ChatGPT will generate a summary of the provided text.
3. "define" - ChatGPT will provide a definition of the provided word or phrase.
4. "translate" - ChatGPT will provide a translation of the provided text.
5. "list" - ChatGPT will generate a list of items based on the provided prompt.

Special Words for ChatGPT:

1. "person" - When used in a prompt, ChatGPT will replace this special word with a random person's name.
2. "place" - When used in a prompt, ChatGPT will replace this special word with a random place name.
3. "time" - When used in a prompt, ChatGPT will replace this special word with a random time.
4. "year" - When used in a prompt, ChatGPT will replace this special word with a random year.
"number" - When used in a prompt, ChatGPT will replace this special word with a random number.

Promptcraft in Canva

Promptcraft is for all ages, not just for experienced writers or professionals. Forming prompts for generative media can open up a world of creative writing and improve critical thinking and editorial skills. Prompt writing and generative tools can provide a structured approach to writing and ideation while developing coherent outlines for projects. Whether you are a beginner or an experienced writer, experimentation in promptcraft can improve the diversity and clarity of thought.

If you are a teacher considering how to use these tools, consider project-based objectives with many tools used over iterations. Combine assignment types over time.

EXERCISES FOR CREATIVE PROMPTCRAFT

- Start by taking a boring prompt, such as "Describe your daily routine," and add a twist to it. For example, "Describe your daily routine as if you were a superhero late for the thing." Think about what makes for a funny or unusual mix of more than 2 items or concepts.
- Take a popular idea or world and use it as inspiration for a prompt. For example, "Write a scene with A and B character set in my world as a baby is being born" Include details that make the scene funny or unusual to fit the theme or mood, such as a Baby Shower card.
- Be imaginative and ask people to share something from a different time period or place. For example, "Write a diary entry as if you were a pirate in the 1700s." Note that in some generators, you'll write year 1706 or similarly detailed timeline to improve language and generator believability for alternate time frames or epochs.
- Use a random word generator to come up with a silly or funny prompt. For example, "Write a short story using the words 'banana', 'umbrella', and 'zombie'."
- Get creative with the format of your prompt. Instead of asking for a traditional essay or story, ask people to write a poem, a song, or a script. Be unique with the format.
- Have fun! The most interesting prompts are the ones that make people laugh, think or both. Create a new context or juxtapose two or more things to make new comparisons.

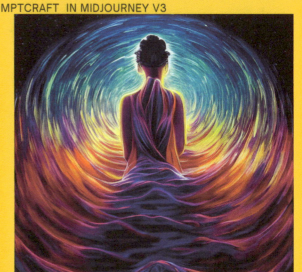

CHARACTERS
DESIGNING ACROSS TOOLS

Another way to use generative text prompts is create new characters. For example, a writer might use a prompt such as "A woman from a mysterious island in the 1800s" to create a new character for a story, give her a name and illustrate her life. The writer can then use this prompt as a starting point for image generation, building a backstory and personality that fit within the context of the prompt. In this case, a woman from the 1800s who would have never been photographed by a camera can be seen in a new way for a new story and world.

"Magic Write is a unique technology"
OR IS IT?
Use Critical Thinking

Promptcraft guidebook exercise

Magic Write 101, Written by Magic Write in Canva

Explain how Canva's Magic Write empowers creators to write docs faster and with fewer errors

Canva's Magic Write is a great tool for any creator looking to write documents faster and with fewer errors. This feature uses AI-powered writing assistance to help you craft a perfect document in no time. Magic Write will suggest words and phrases as you type, helping you to make fewer spelling and grammar mistakes. It also provides real-time feedback on your writing style and structure, allowing you to make corrections quickly. In addition, you can use the thesaurus to find the right words to express your ideas. All these features combined make it easier for creators to write documents faster and with fewer errors.

Describe the technology that drives Magic Write in Canva

Magic Write is a unique technology built by Canva that uses artificial intelligence to help you create beautiful content quickly and easily. It utilizes natural language processing to detect the context of what you're writing and suggests relevant images, text, and design elements that can be used to enhance the look and feel of your content. It also has a built-in spellchecker to help you avoid errors, and it can even suggest ideas for improving the overall design and layout of your content. With Magic Write, you can create stunning visuals in Canva without having to worry about design or layout, allowing you to focus on creating great content.

Evo Heyning
Just now

Is this true, was it built internally?

Note: Always edit! Check for errors. Screenshot provided for workflow process.
Most text generators are not accurate 100% of the time and require research.

Magic Write 101
Written by Magic Write in Canva

PROMPT: Explain how Canva's Magic Write empowers creators to write docs faster and with fewer errors

Canva's Magic Write is a great tool for any creator looking to write documents faster and with fewer errors. This feature uses AI-powered writing assistance to help you craft a perfect document in no time. Magic Write will suggest words and phrases as you type, helping you to make fewer spelling and grammar mistakes. It also provides real-time feedback on your writing style and structure, allowing you to make corrections quickly. In addition, you can use the thesaurus to find the right words to express your ideas. All these features combined make it easier for creators to write documents faster and with fewer errors.

Evo's Notes: Canva is fair to fine for international business use cases such as technical writing docs, brand and asset management or internal training. It is not creative or useful for fiction as it will be for non-fiction business writing. This page took 15 minutes to assemble, quite a bit faster than the average time per page of 30 minutes of writing/editing for this book. The snippet in white above was not edited to compare the writing quality of Canva to ChatGPT and other tools

Consider complex media generation assignments

MEDIA GENERATION

18
A billion new novels will be published by bots? Not unless they're prompted to do it.

12
EXCERPT:
REALITYCRAFT
SERIES

9
AUTHOR SPOTLIGHT:
Evo Heyning using
Canva & Diffusion Tools

Try writing a sample journal, book or other complex publication

Bend your brain around it

Try the weirdest words you can think of to spark unusual new ideas

2
Editor's Note

CONTENTS

7
Getting Started with Promptcraft

20
Introduction to Generative Media

What is Generative Media?

Benefits of Generative Media

Choosing the Right Tools

Tips for Creating Generative Media
Creating Quality Content

Optimizing Your Generative Media
Common Issues & Solutions

Resources for Open Development

Realitycraft Community
Thank You

TXT2BFD

Exclusive Excerpt!

How to Write a Blog Post in Less than 5 Minutes

Book Generation

EMERGING IDEAS IN HAND

Prompt Often, Edit Like A Beast

EXPERIMENTAL NOISE

How many fingers is too many, anyway?

EXERCISES TO TRY &

Prompt the tool to come up with a new character and ask for details about their life, including their name and backstory. Keep generating until that backstory feels like a whole character vs. a flat one-dimensional trope.

Prompt for sample story arcs, plotlines and expand on your worldbuilding, then save that work to your favorite worldbuilding tool for sharing with your team or tracking those elements through design and into production.

The "craft" portion of promptcraft includes using your curiosity, words & inquiry to generate new and exciting writing ideas. **Be inspired to be inspiring.** Whether you are a fiction writer, poet, tech writer, playwright or screenwriter, promptcraft can help you to expand your idea base. By working with your prompts and iterating you can unlock new creative potential and explore new writing techniques or types of characters over time.

Prompts come in many different forms, from simple word lists to complex story starters. These starters operate like sourdough starter in baking to grow and generate ideas for fiction, poetry, plays, screenplays and more. Some prompts are designed to inspire a specific type of writing, such as a short story or a poem, while others are more open-ended and can be used for any type of writing.

FEED THE BOOKWORM

Make Writing Less Manual

Promptcraft can be used to overcome writers block. When faced with a blank page, it can be difficult to know where to begin. Prompts can provide a starting point for your writing and can help you to overcome the fear of the blank page. Try asking for a list of related items for a scene or use juxtapositions in prompts to generate new and exciting writing ideas and get your creative juices flowing.

Promptcraft in Midjourney V4   Try a 3 Word Prompt like Confused, Surrealist, Dripping

For fiction and creative writing, generative media tools are a powerful tool for overcoming creative blocks and pushing past artistic boundaries. Tools like Scenario.gg, ChatGPT, Playground.AI, Jasper.AI or DreamStudio allow artists to create unusual and unpredictable results, giving them a sense of freedom and inspiration that can be difficult to find in traditional art forms. Try these tips for using generative media tools to overcome creative blocks and push past artistic boundaries.

LANGUAGE
TIPS FOR PROMPTCRAFT

USE VERBS

Describe, Explain

Enumerate, List

KEEP IT SIMPLE

Fewer articles, focus on

nouns, adjectives, the big

question or discovery

LEAD THE QUERY

Ask for what you need

specifically with constraints

Ever Ask About Its Rules?

Here's the response generated from ChatGPT as *Best Rules for Promptcraft.*

When writing a prompt, it's important to:

1. **Keep it clear and concise:** Make sure the prompt is easy to understand and gets straight to the point.
2. **Be specific**: Be as specific as possible about what you're asking for, so that the responder can give a focused and relevant answer.
3. **Avoid bias**: Try to avoid language or questions that could be seen as biased or leading.
4. **Consider your audience**: Think about who will be reading or responding to the prompt and tailor it accordingly.
5. **Proofread**: Always proofread and edit your prompt for grammar and spelling errors before sending it out.

Evo's Notes: Often the first generation from ChatGPT is not great. This isn't fully relevant to the specifics of generative media and may be based on very generic information about prompting. Regenerate and try again.

Regen: Ask It to Try Again?

Here's the response generated from ChatGPT as Best Rules for Promptcraft on the second regeneration. Iteration is everything. Capitalization errors surprisingly came from ChatGPT.

Here are a few tips for writing a great prompt for a generative media tool:

1. Be specific and clear about what you want the model to generate.
2. Provide enough context for the model to understand the task at hand.
3. Use concrete examples to help the model understand what you're looking for.
4. Avoid using overly complex or technical language that the model may not understand.
5. Be creative and have fun with it!
6. test the prompt with different input and adjust accordingly.
7. Be mindful of the length of the prompt and make sure it is not too long or too short.

Evo's Notes: Even the second generation from ChatGPT is not perfect. This needs an edit. Regenerate and try again.

Tell me step by step how do you write a great prompt for ChatGPT

1. Start with a clear and specific topic or question: Your prompt should be focused and well-defined, so that ChatGPT knows what information or response you are looking for.

2. Provide context and background information: If the topic is complex or unfamiliar, provide some background information to help ChatGPT understand the context.

3. Use natural language: Write your prompt in a clear and natural language, avoiding jargon or technical terms.

4. Be concise: Keep your prompt short and to the point, so that ChatGPT can quickly understand what you want.

5. Test your prompt: Test your prompt by inputting it into ~~ChatGPT~~ *NO* and checking the response to make sure it is accurate and relevant.

6. Give it a try with different variations, different contexts and different types of responses.

7. Have fun and get creative with it, You can also use multiple prompts to generate a story, a dialogue or even a song.

Managing Attributions & Copy Uses

EVO HEYNING — Human Creator

Catgems at Realitycraft — Title, Series

December 2022
Made with
Midjourney and
Scenario.gg

Digital Illustration with
Generators & Algo Tools
(Media Used in Creation)

New Uses that Transform Media

Note: There is no one accepted attribution format yet and this is a suggested approach for relevant generative images. Please consider how attribution helps to tell your media story.

Digital Media Attribution of Assets Report

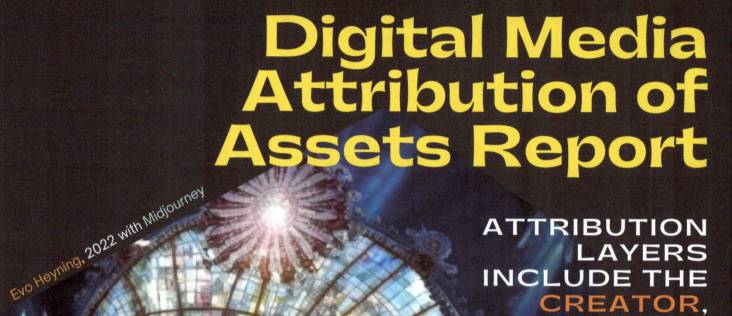

Evo Heyning, 2022 with Midjourney

ATTRIBUTION LAYERS INCLUDE THE CREATOR, MEDIA ASSIST & YEAR OF WORK

Digital Illustration by Evo Heyning in Midjourney

Note that laws around attribution including listing where AI tools are used are rapidly evolving. Consult your local authorities for rules where you live.

AUTHENTICITY IS stunning

"GenAI's will improve the overall look, feel, speed, and cost of things.

And lazy prompt building or high volume generation will result in a great deal of "perfect" and "elegant" content — that will begin to feel the same.

Right now, it's very exciting and fresh, but once we all know that its machine generated it will begin to land less and less.

What will capture your attention, will be imperfectly perfect humans.

Technology is like water.

Water is fully integrated with life. It is neither bad nor good – it is both.

In this new digital age, you must be a swimmer, able to swim in the ocean of technology.

Too much water. You drown.

Too little water. You dehydrate and fall behind.

Surely, swimming with GenAI means becoming an expert PromptBuilder.

It also means that to stand out in any way, for any reason, you must discover who you really are.

Authenticity will matter more and more."

• **Nichol Bradford**   Transtech Lab, Niremia Collective

STORIES

Start with

WORLDBUILDING

APPLYING GENERATIVE
MEDIA TOOLS TO DESIGN &
MAKE NEW WORLDS

—

Worldbuilding is the process of creating a fictional universe and the rules that govern it. This can include creating characters, locations, cultures, and history for a story or game or as seen here, concepts for an XR or 3D immersive world on the web to serve as a research library and guild.

Prompts can be used to play out ideas for worldbuilding; this is a part of concept design. For example, a prompt such as "a world where animals have evolved to be the dominant species" could inspire a person to create a society where animals hold political power and humans are subservient. Text generators can provide some of those potential storylines but will need heavy editing before being ready to produce.

Generative media tools can also be used to create and regenerate elements of a world on trained models. Naming the characters, describing the settings, outlining potential story plotlines and exploring the detailed workings of that world can all happen through ChatGPT by asking for a script in the style you are looking for or by building a model to run expansive simulations in advanced metaverse and XR platforms such as those from NVIDIA or Microsoft for AI & hardware integration.

To organize your elements into games, stories and campaigns consider tools like **World Anvil**, a worldbuilding tool that provides templates for creating characters, locations, cultures, and plotlines. It allows users to organize and share their worldbuilding information for play. **Scenario.gg** is a tool used to train original models based on your previous generations for worldbuilding related to games including everything you'd find in a game, from characters to gems and background assets.

GEN*TIPS

Tip 1: Experiment with many different generative media tools

Each tool has its own set of features and capabilities, so it is important to explore different options to find the ones that work best for you. There are over a dozen in this book to try from Scenario.gg to HeyFriday, ChatGPT and Stable Diffusion.

Tip 2: Use generative media tools to create a starting point

Example, you can use a generative media tool to create a random palette, pattern or shape, and then use that as a starting point for your painting or sculpture. This iterative ideation can help to break the creative block and give you a sense of direction for your artwork - use multiple image prompts in Midjourney to try blending your works and ideas.

Tip 3: Remix! Combine generative media tools with your old art forms

Try blending your previous art with new generative works -- use your favorite generative media tool to create a digital image using one of your old pieces or ideas, and then use that image as the basis for an Augie video. Remix your works into new media. This can help to break the creative block and give you a sense of direction for your artwork or worldbuilding project.

Tip 4: Use generative media tools to explore new styles & techniques

Experiment with a generative media tools in different styles to create a digital image, and then use that image as the basis for a painting or sculpture. You can use sites like Playground.AI or Lexica.art to explore the work of others to get inspired with new ideas and promptcraft riffs. This can help to break the creative block and give you a sense of direction for your artwork.

Tip 5: Use gens to create a sense of unpredictability and expansiveness

Parameters like --chaos and style worlds, even emoji can create a sense of mystery and unpredictability that may surprise and delight you in the process of making new works. If you're stuck in a rut, switch it up and try an emoji or borrow a riff and remix it with your own secret sauce and flavor. Think about the 20 words that define your work and always expand on it.

VIDEO GENERATION

NVIDIA

AugXLabs

This section will be detailed second edition as new video tools become available for the public. You can sign up for the beta of AugxLabs tool Augie to try something today or make an avatar video in a tool like Synthesia.

SYNTHESIA

GOOGLE

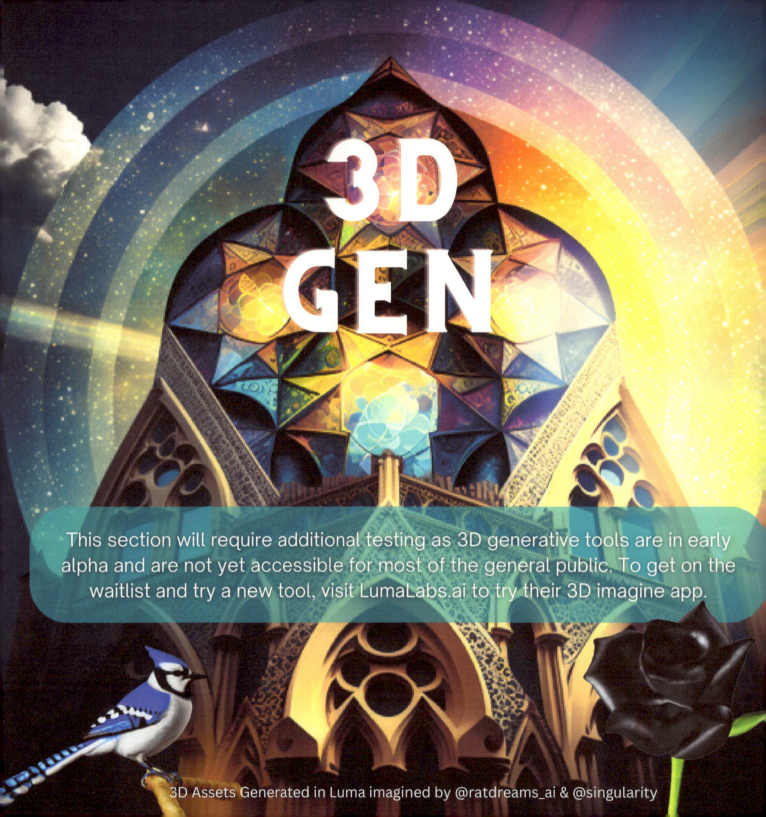

3D GEN

This section will require additional testing as 3D generative tools are in early alpha and are not yet accessible for most of the general public. To get on the waitlist and try a new tool, visit LumaLabs.ai to try their 3D imagine app.

3D Assets Generated in Luma imagined by @ratdreams_ai & @singularity

Text to 4D

A corgi playing with a ball.

A panda dancing.

A space shuttle launching.

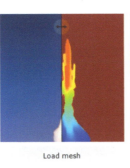

Clown fish swimming through the coral reef.

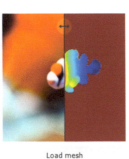

MAV3D

MakeAVideo3D, now out on Github and in early papers, shows how 4D text to video prompting works

Load mesh   Load mesh   Load mesh   Load mesh

An emoji of a baby panda reading a book.

A dog riding a skateboard.

3D rendering of a fox playing videogame.

A squirrel riding a motorcycle.

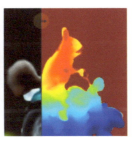

Image-to-4D   *Note: This tool will be reviewed in a future version of Promptcraft.*

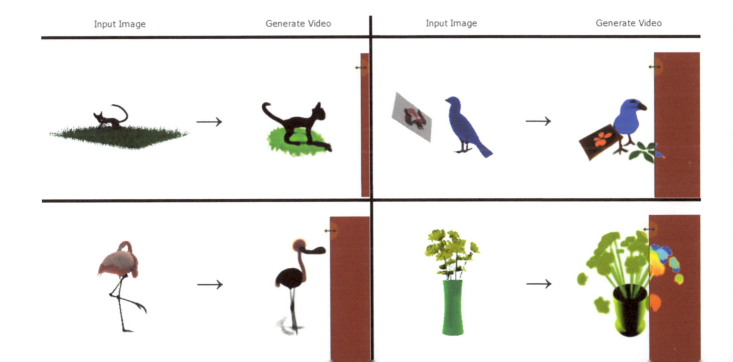

FLOORING

UPSTAIRS WALLPAPER

DOWNSTAIRS WALLPAPER

AI FLOORING CREATOR

Now Creating: "Black chinoserie gilt lacquerware"

Please wait. Our AI friend is doing its thing...

LOADING...

SIMULACRA.IO

FLOORING

3D Generative tools like Simulacra.io from REM5 allow for a social generative experience for Fashion, Architecture or Collaboration

SHIRT

AI FASHION CREATOR - SHIRT

Current Human Prompt: "California poppy superbloom"

Type here. Describe anything you'd like to see.

CREATE   SAVE CURRENT IMAGE

SIMULACRA   **SIMULACRA.IO**

HELMET

SHIRT

AI FASHION CREATOR - HELMET

Current Human Prompt: "Poppy flower up close"

Type here. Describe anything you'd like to see...

CREATE   SAVE CURRENT IMAGE

Some creators are working around the
challenges in accessible 3D generative
tooling by developing their own coded
assets for Blender using ChatGPT.

Hybrid approaches continue to
stimulate new development and
innovation across fields for
interoperability and open development
of worlds. This will be explored in the
next book in this series, Realitycraft.

ChatGPT to
BLENDER

NEXT EXPERIMENTS

**GENERATIVE CODE
TO 3D DESIGN &
METAVERSE DEV**

Experiment with New & Impossible Architectures

Generative tools do not replace the creative life - they superpower it. If used well, generative media tools enable everyone to be more creative, experimental and prolific.

TOOLS TO TRY FOR ADVANCED EXPERIMENTAL PROMPTCRAFT

PLAYGROUND.AI

SIMULACRA.IO

SCENARIO.GG

AugXLabs/AUGIE

RUNWAY.ML

HUGGING FACE

HEY FRIDAY

BLUEWILLOW

FERMAT

JASPER.AI

COPY.AI

WOMBO ART

FUTUREPEDIA

MAGIC WRITE*
Write 5 tips to better promptcraft in Canva

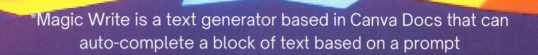

*Magic Write is a text generator based in Canva Docs that can auto-complete a block of text based on a prompt

Create a theme for your prompts. This will help you stay organized and give your prompts a consistent feel.

Make sure your prompts are easy to read and understand. Use clear, concise language and break up long paragraphs into smaller chunks.

Incorporate visuals into your prompts.
Gens offer many great design tools and
resources that can help give your
prompts a fresh look.

Think outside the box! Challenge yourself to come up with new and creative ideas for your prompts.

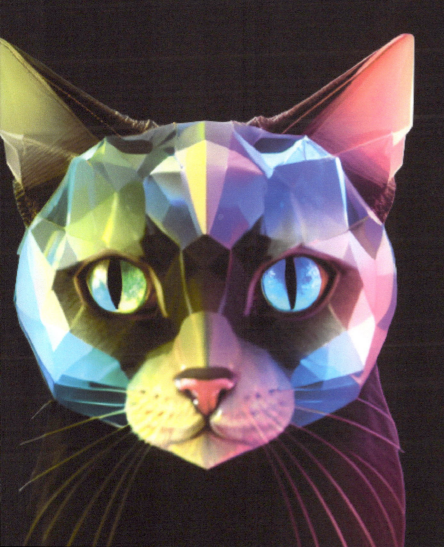

Have fun! Writing is a creative process and can be enjoyable. Experiment and have fun with it.

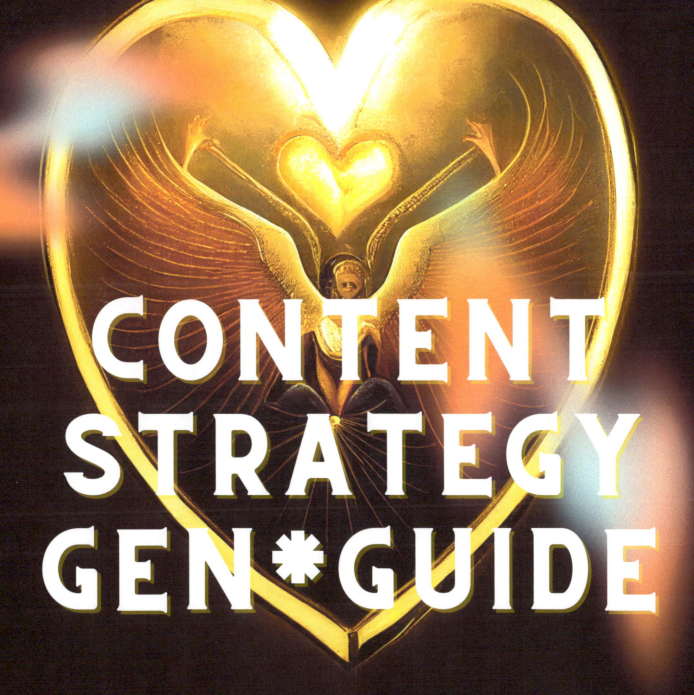

Note: This section is designed for anyone deciding how to use these tools for strategy work with teams or to deliver on goals at the workplace. Feel free to use these suggestions in your strategy dashboard and tools of choice, especially tools like Notion where generative prompts may be baked into the interface for content and strategy planning with your team.

How to use these tools at work: Template for Generative Content Strategy Planning

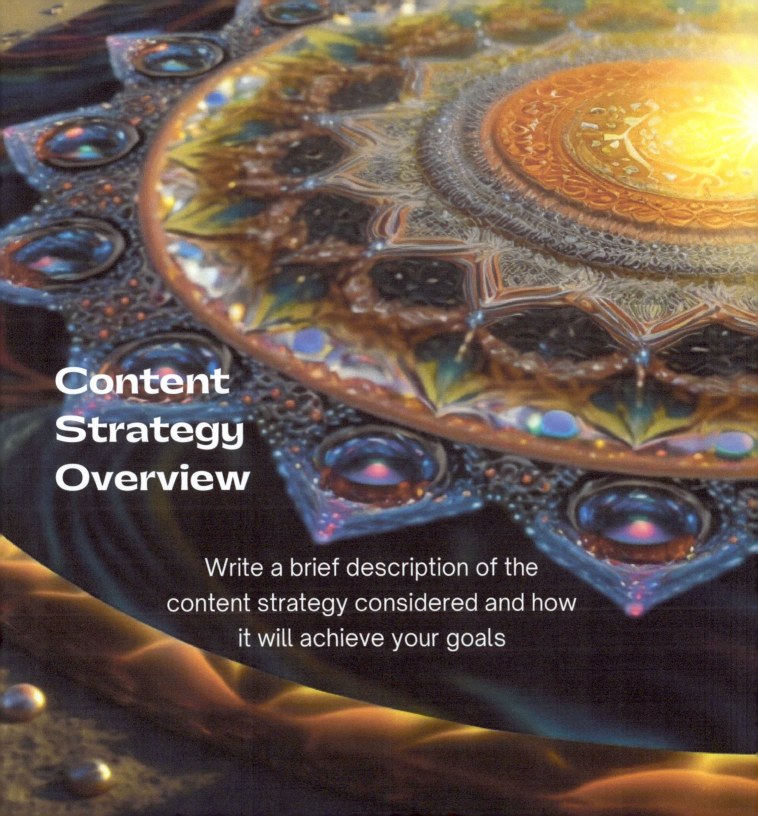

Content Strategy Overview

Write a brief description of the content strategy considered and how it will achieve your goals

STRATEGY
Goal: Publish eBook & Course

GENERATION DURATION:	Plan for a period of time including enough time for iterations (plural) on generative work from first promptcraft through editing cycles and publishing
CONTENT PREPARED BY:	Add the name of the team or the lead content strategist and list roles for team as needed for editorial and creative support staff

Listing your aspirations form the basis of your content strategy, making it easier for your team to link back promptcraft strategies to the company's bigger mission. Develop a cluster of keywords for your descriptor and make note of any words related to brand, tone, style & palette.

- List creative or business goals here

- Add descriptive clusters of words for prompts

- Add style words that speak to your identity

Prompt to your Audiences

	Audience 1: Creatives at Work	Audience 2: Technologists Experimenting
Demographics Age range Gender Occupation Choose words, ideas, tone that will resonate with your audiences	25-34 years old More women than men Senior Creatives, Designers, Directors Needs to Streamline Costs & Be Efficient for Creative Work	18-75 Balanced genders/fluid Experienced, Senior Tech Willing to Spend to Experiment & Create
Psychographics Lifestyle Hobbies Values	Urban dweller, vibrant, active Decorating, fashion and cooking Career-oriented, family and spiritual Interested in creative realization	Nomadic, Global, Digital Native Creative Technologists Family & Friends Creators Often Closet Artists
Content They Like	Design & decor, art, cats	Tools, how to guides, cats
Communication Platforms They Prefer	Instagram reels, short videos, YouTube first	Technical blog posts, Reddit and Github repos, FOSS & Mastodon

THINK ABOUT WHERE YOUR PROMPTCRAFT WILL LAND AND TRY TO TAILOR YOUR CREATIVE FLOW TO THE INTENDED AUDIENCES

USE TOOLS THAT REFLECT THE INTERESTS, VALUES AND GOALS OF YOUR AUDIENCES

USE YOUR PROMPTCRAFT TO WRITE TO THEM SPECIFICALLY

	Website	eBook	Course
Business Goals	Engage people new to AI and prompt work	Finish lists for the eBook guides that are easy to reuse	Engage active students in deeper coursework
Target Audience	Groups 1&2	Groups 1&2	Group 2 Public, Group 1 at Work
Type of Content	How to guides, Vids, Struggling with writing promps for work? Appeal to creative, effective collab/work	Short useful lists with examples of best words to use with illustrative images and screenshots	Short videos for async coursework on promptcraft for business, make it easy after hours learning experimentation
Content Platforms	Generative email & images	Generative copy	Live with vid clips
Key Performance Indicators (KPI)	Open email and conversion rate, posts shared	Sales of eBook, reviews, Audio downloads	Views on YouTube, sales of courses
Resources	Copy.ai, Jasper.ai	ChatGPT, Midjourney	Augie, AugXLabs

DESIGN EDITORIAL TO MEET THE NEEDS OF YOUR LEGAL TEAMS AS WELL AS YOUR CONTENT & CREATIVE TEAM

Marketing materials are an important part of any business and text generators like ChatGPT can be used to generate text for a variety of marketing materials including brochures, flyers and ads.

Some examples of ChatGPT text prompts for marketing materials include:

- "Write a brochure for a new product"
- "Create a flyer for a upcoming event"
- "Generate an advertisement for a sale"

Social Media Posts and entire campaigns can be quickly written in Copy.AI, Canva or HeyFriday, just add your descriptors for useful outcomes.

Cats Slaying a Midjourney Catwalk

Use your Design Programs to Organize Assets

streamline**styleguide**

Curate data sets & collections to use in new models after editing and branding

CONSIDER USE OF
CREATIVE SUITES & TOOLS
FROM DESIGN COMPANIES
LIKE CANVA, ADOBE &
NVIDIA WITH YOUR OPEN
SOURCE GENERATIVE
TOOLS TO ORGANIZE

PRINTED GIVEAWAYS

Generative media such as images can work well as printed giveaway items bespoke to the event, the product, the customer or the audience at large. Try words related to the type of item you want to design

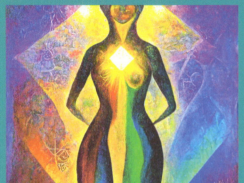

APP DOWNLOADS

Be clear and make sure any assets you choose to generate will work for the types of deliveries you intend to produce, for example web & app friendly graphics vs. print or video production quality media

BOOK PUBLISHING

Images (and text) generated from tools require extensive upscaling, editing, remixing, iteration and preparation before being ready for books or any sort of printed objects, especially at largest scale

Delivering Products

TIMELINES

SCHEDULE ITERATIVE GENERATIVE FLOW WITH YOUR CREATIVE TEAMS

USE CASE: PROMPTCRAFT SERIES FROM COURSE & EBOOK THROUGH SERIES

PROMPTCRAFT REALITYCRAFT SERIES EVO HEYNING

JANUARY 2023

Promptcraft Courses generative tests, game testing, **eBook** to print, generative output through editing process, 4 weeks, thousands of images & concepts, scripts and ideas, editing

FEBRUARY 2023

Testing the **Advanced Topics coursework** weekly, development of Promptcraft wiki and resource guides open source, community testing for experience design and play

MARCH 2023

Iterate the coursework and **Book** to update with new tools and resources, add to the **wiki** and share 4-6 **video** interviews with CEOs of generative media tools, human to human with generative bumpers

SUMMER 2023

Realitycraft Guide for World creation and designing the futures of your dreams - series publishing of 3 books, videos and courses, banked assets >100,000

Note: While your timelines to produce new works will shorten, the iteration cycles can remain long if you need approvals from many different people. Try to experiment, work nimbly and include collaborators as soon as you can to get the most well-rounded results for your team.

Augies = Generative Vids Now in Beta

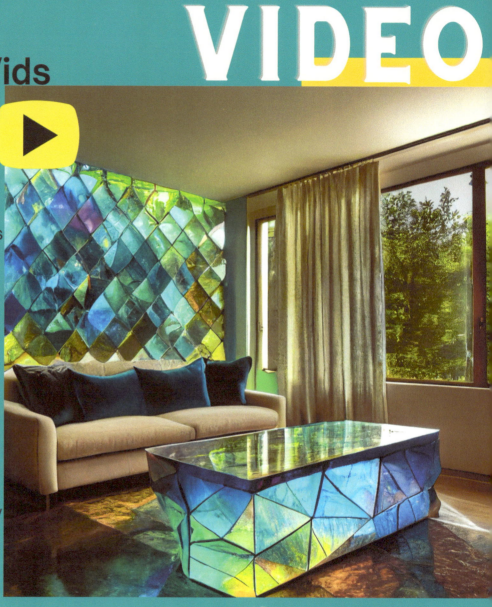

Prompts can also be used in a wide variety of video generation topics - and this technology is it in its early stages. While companies like NVIDIA have provided StyleGAN tools to industry at higher cost for years, lower cost democratized creative generators will take some time to build extensive capacities for generative video. As that happens, companies like AugXLabs will lead the way with Augies, short generative videos from a script or upload.

VIDEO

PRODUCTION

WORKFLOWS

How this Plays Out in the Workplace with Generative Media

DETERMINE HOW & WHERE TO PUBLISH

Not every arena is ready for generative work. Is yours? Clear your path for production with colleagues

MAKE SURE YOUR CREATIVE PLAN MATCHES YOUR GOALS

Confirm your promptcraft matches your strategy & goal

CLEAR YOUR WORK WITH CREATIVE TEAM

Others on your team may catch mistakes you may miss. Remember to edit everything that comes out of a generator

Note: this is the image quality of a first generation. Upscaling removes the noise and improves quality for printing. Printed media will want max upscale before printing to reduce artifacts.

UPSCALE!

promptcraft guidebook

imagined ideas

Generative Remixes of Worlds That Never Existed

These were never paintings on a wall but they may look like it

Is it a Fair Use?

Diffusion models, which are used to generate new content based on existing media in trained models, can present challenges now being considered on copyright, intellectual property and fair use of art and media in AI models. One major issue currently under consideration will determine whether the generated content is considered a derivative work, which would require permission from the original copyright holder. Additionally, the use of images, videos, and audio in AI models may also raise questions about fair use and the rights of the creators and owners of that content.

Please consult your advisors; none of this is legal advice.

It's important for developers and creators using AI models to be aware of these legal and ethical issues and to take steps to ensure that they are not infringing on the rights of others. This may include obtaining permission from copyright holders, using royalty-free or public domain content and implementing systems to detect and remove infringing content. Note that most generative media content may not be able to be copywritten as generated and any work will need extensive editing and recreation by hand after the generative process. Human labor is always engaged in these creative works.

Promptcraft in Canva

Time will tell.

Share, Iterate &
Keep Experimenting

Visit groups like the Realitycraft groups to be inspired by the experiments of others and try new words, styles, ideas and tools that may be out of your comfort zone. Combining media can sometimes yield outstanding results. Your mileage will always vary.

PROMPTCRAFT IN MIDJOURNEY: ART NOUVEAU POSTER

ARTICULATE YOUR DESIGN BRIEF
USE THAT INQUIRY TO FORM THE PROMPT
ITERATE, VARIATE,
UPSCALE, REMIX, REPEAT

Production Strategy & Planning Notes

Speed up the time of production by generating and banking content to keep on hand and use in your editorial calendar and production workflows throughout the campaign or year. This content is also useful for training your copy and image models internally for future use.

Expect the number of collaborators to add weeks to generative approval and editing process. Editing of collections from first generative content through to publishing can take anywhere from 1 hour to 1 quarter depending on number of people engaged and how many editorial passes are required to produce.

Advanced production workflows may involve generating, editing, training and re-prompting on thousands of images for every scene in a game or story world. To manage these workflows, hire a prompt engineer who can work with your team to train models and refine internal promptcraft processes with an eye toward cohesive media and content development.

EVO'S SECRET RECIPES

BEAUTY FULL PROMPTCRAFT

Promptcraft in Canva: Breakfast, eggs, bacon, toast, delicious morning complete meal at breakfast

Creativity can be defined as the ability to generate novel and valuable ideas and the process of turning those ideas into reality. Prompting fosters creativity by shifting the context, language or constraints in which a task or problem is presented, opening up new options.

Your special sauce will have a different flavor than others.

By carefully choosing the prompts, tools and inquiries used to inspire or guide creative thinking, it is possible to increase the likelihood of generating novel and useful ideas. If your idea isn't working in one place, try the same prompt elsewhere. Remix. Iterate.

EVO'S FAVORITE PROMPTCRAFT RECIPE

INGREDIENTS

Media Design

Context

Product or Content Idea

Descriptive Input

Parameters and Modifiers

Original Art, Media or Sketches

Remixable Seed & Spicy Language for Flavor

STEPS

1
Write down the keywords that describe your concept with as few additional words as possible

2
Start your prompt phrase with a context such as a design product or output goal with a clear sense of design brief

3
Include any modifiers that describe the palette, world, background, style of artistry or conceptual curveballs to add complexity to your prompt

4
Generate rounds of media until you are excited by the outcomes and then take that media out to be refined through your workflow

5
Remix and repeat hundreds of times and edit judiciously until ready for publication

Promptcraft in Midjourney: Transparent architecture, modern design

GALLERY MANAGEMENT

Organize assets for remixing

DESIGNERS TIPS FOR CREATING BODIES OF WORK

Save and upload each collection into a resource you can train for future models and asset development

Use your collection tools wisely to track internal assets for creative remixing and training

Midjourney collections can assist with finding generative works months later for remixing

Google Photos & Drive are lower cost for independent creators along with Canva, Notion, open source tools

At the Realitycraft gallery and design lab in Oakland, CA every step of this Promptcraft and Realitycraft process is a game, an experiment, a design lab taking place in a physical gallery for generative creativity

Through a mix of workshops, salons, design sessions and work with physical art, antiques and treasures we build new types of worlds inspired by the most beautiful artistry and creative works of all time. *This Realitycraft process will be explored in an upcoming book of this series, coming summer of 2023.*

dream
Canva
 OpenAI

Share your
Experiences
and Discoveries
___

GITHUB
Promptcraft Resource Wiki

FACEBOOK
Realitycraft Group

INSTAGRAM
#Promptcraft to share your stories

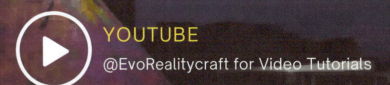
YOUTUBE
@EvoRealitycraft for Video Tutorials

For events, workshops, art & stories
visit <u>evo.ist</u>

evo

A book on world creation   By Evo Heyning   Coming in

2023

REALITYCRAFT

Visit Realitycraft on YouTube for more of the workshop clips & content

EVO.IST

LIKE

& SUBSCRIBE

METAVERSE AI
REALITYCRAFT
DESIGN LAB

from: EVO
to: READERS

THANK YOU FOR YOUR INSIGHTS!

YOU ARE WELCOME TO JOIN THE REALITYCRAFT GALLERY & DESIGN LAB GROUP TO SHARE YOUR EXPERIMENTS

Evo

COMING IN 2023

REALITYCRAFT
SURREALIST PORTRAITURE
REIMAGINED ANCIENT ARTIFACES

EVO.IST